PICTURE
MAKER

AN AUTOBIOGRAPHY

PETER ETRIL SNYDER

The title of this book describes how I see myself. I called myself a painter until, at a garden party, a woman that I had just met asked me to paint her house. I do mean paint her house. Clearly, I had to change my answer to questions about my occupation. Picture-maker describes what I am and what I enjoy. I am one of those fortunate few that actually has earned his living from what he enjoys most. I will leave you to decide what art is and who is an artist.

Often people seem incredulous when they find I have little emotional attachment to my paintings. Those people splash me with stories of creators who cannot bear to part with their works. They hold on to pieces for many years, moving them from house to house or studio to studio as they progress through life. That seems a little sad to me. It is almost as if they feel that they will lose a bit of themselves if they set their paintings free. I have a different view for two reasons. First, my interest in my painting is in the doing, the act of making the pictures. When one work is done, there remains a growing army of paintings in my mind waiting for marching orders. The number of these paintings-in-waiting increases the longer I live. I see new things or old things in a new way and wish to deal with them. I find such fun, such joy, such immediate satisfaction in developing a painting. Even if a painting is not successful, I can draw satisfaction from small areas of it. I think most painters recognize that time in the making of a painting when you turn the corner and realize just what is necessary to complete that work. For me that is especially true as I do not work from a carefully scripted plan. I approach a painting with a general idea, and then in painting the work I develop a fuller realization of that idea. I like to think at the end of a painting I am a bit smarter than I was when I started. It is true that my method means a lot of frustration when I cannot pull the design together. It is true that this approach results in many unfinished, unresolved paintings. It is also true that to paint this way, each painting becomes a trial. However, when a painting does coalesce the satisfaction is enormous. At the risk of sounding too Zen, I really feel a duel or contest with the painting as a stroke that I make brings to my mind fresh opportunities unthought of before. The second reason to set my paintings free is to spread that satisfaction to a viewer. A man from the Kingston area told me that after living with one of my paintings in his home he totally changed his appreciation of light and its effects. He told me how his vision of the ordinary had come alive. That conversation took place twelve years ago, but I can hear it still. The old question "If a tree falls in the woods, if no one hears it does it make a sound" is, I think, equally true of painting. If no one sees my painting I may as well be playing solitaire. That approach holds no joy for me. Because all a picture-maker has to offer is his personality, I will try in this book to describe my working journey with reference to my personal history and those people and events that shaped me. I've just finished reading an autobiography by a famous lawyer and was sorry that at the end I liked him less than I had before I started reading his story. Inevitably, I will bore some readers in areas of my life or work that hold no interest for them. I include what I do in an attempt to be straightforward and plain spoken. For those who know me well that will come as no surprise. I believe that confusion can arise even when people attempt to be direct. It will be necessary to leave a lot out. Just as in painting, I will attempt to show my point of view by focusing on information that I think important and ignoring extraneous detail. As I wrote this book I realized three distinct stages in my work. In the first stage I tried to paint things the way I thought they were. With time and training I developed to the second stage. I learned how to really look and describe. It was in that stage that I painted things the way they were. Now, at this stage of my journey, I realize that I am painting things the way I wish them to be. I carefully shape the subject to my aesthetic point of view. I have no idea how long this approach will last. Perhaps I will move to another point of view, perhaps just develop within this frame. It will depend on opportunities and influences I meet. I am curious to see just what I will do next.

I believe very strongly that all a picture-maker has to offer to the public is his point of view, his personality. It would be impossible for me to describe myself without telling you about my wife Marilyn. She has been the biggest influence on my life. We were married very young, she was twenty, I was twenty-two. Although we are descended from similar Mennonite backgrounds we shared an appreciation of aesthetics even before we knew what that really meant. To say that we came from a void where the visual arts are concerned is not an overstatement. Marilyn's exposure to literature from a degree in English and my training at art college meant that we influenced each other. Our travel to Britain was encouraged by those twin interests. Because we have no children, we have always spent a good deal of time together. For most people our closeness would, probably, be too much. For us, this close combination seems to work. In 1981 Marilyn went to Ontario College of Art in Toronto to study design with an eye on fibre art as a specialty. She graduated, something I never did, only to find that she really did not want to pursue weaving. It was so fortunate for me that she received that art college training. She is able to understand in such a strong way the difficulties of painting. Painting is a lovely pursuit. As an artist I must march to my own drummer to develop visual ideas. It is wonderful to have a wife who understands the process.

Hidcote, a renowned English garden, is the setting for this photo of Marilyn. She enjoys herself so much at English gardens and it shows (left).

For our twenty-fifth wedding anniversary Marilyn and I travelled to England on the Queen Elizabeth 2. On the way home we took the Concorde. It was a fast return but not terribly exciting (above right).

Several years ago we attended an event which was very popular. People ended up standing in ranks several deep to observe the action. A very tall man with a shorter wife stood behind his wife. "I can see over her" he said, "but she can see through me." That also works at our house.

As I get older I am much more aware of life style than I was as a young man. I now jealously guard the amount of time and energy that I spend on non-painting activities. Marilyn's slower natural rhythm has helped me to calm down. Instinctively my reaction time to a stimulus is almost immediate. Over the years I have seen how much better it is to have a more considered reaction. I have learned that to be reflective it is necessary to have quiet time. Not for us the constant movement and endless social round that is the norm for a lot of people. I think it is quite probable that most long-married couples have influenced each other a great deal. It is not, however, until I attempt to write about Marilyn's effect on me that I realize just how extensive it has been. I owe her much on so many levels from her aesthetic sense to her love of words. Once again the fortunes have favoured me.

A photo of we three Snyder boys taken in our garden at Water Street in Waterloo. Already my mom must have realized that I was going to be an artist. Check the beret!

My strongest childhood impression is one of boredom. My mother was a very nervous person who felt somewhat out of place in town. Both sides of my family had been farmers for hundreds of years. When my father and his brother, Mel, came to town to run a dairy, they were among the first of our group of Mennonites to live their lives off the farm. True, my great-grandfather Snyder retired to Waterloo, but he had farmed on what is now Fischer-Hallman Road. I am delighted that when I look out the east side of my Erb Street gallery I can see his retirement house. My father never seemed to be concerned by this uprooting from the farm. He worked fatiguingly long hours, although he did not seem to tire. In the late 1940's and early 50's our dairy, Maple Lane Dairy, still had ten horses to pull the laden wagons around Waterloo, and then later, Kitchener as well. The dairy barn stood on a spot near to the current intersection of Regina Street and University Avenue East. Although I enjoyed going to the barn, I did not always enjoy the chores that needed to be done there. Since my twin brothers, Doug and Don, are three years older than I, it fell to them to apply the polish to the harness that dad had draped over a 2x4 hung from the rafters. Since I was so small, I could only rub up the leather. This is a job whose allure very quickly fades. Providing grain to the horses was a job that I could handle and enjoy as a child. There was a sense of power in commanding those gentle giants. As I got a bit older I would sometimes serve as a runner for one of the delivery men who happened to be injured; many trips from milkbox to wagon was the way that game was played. Occasionally in the evening I would accompany my father to the dairy where, in the grimmest of basements, he would count milk tickets and then burn them. As that great furnace opened to swallow the tickets, I thought of Shadrach, Meshach and Abednego.

As a child it seemed to me that I spent all my time either in school or church or obeying my mother. Her overriding fear of what trouble we would get into made her feel best when she controlled the situation. My mom, poor soul, is still alive at eighty-four but because she is quite confused she is in a nursing home where she controls nothing.

I could speculate endlessly if my desire to be without bounds is part of why I was attracted to art at an early age. I first became aware that I was unusual in the area of art when in grade two I, along with only three other kids, was given an oversized paper on which to work. I suppose today a teacher could not show that sort of favouritism but in those days my teacher, a very righteous old lady, Miss MacDonald, could do as she wished. Another thing that she did was to rush to a student who had done an outstanding job on something and kiss them. How embarrassing! However, it seldom happened to me as rarely did I excel. Grade two was my last full year in the old Central School. Part way through the next year, we moved next door to the shiny new MacGregor School. This new school was named for a much acclaimed teacher. Schools tend to be named for teachers or principals. How about naming a school for a graduate? It might draw the kids' attention to successes beyond the school system. Why not an Edna Staebler School here in Waterloo Region? But, I digress.

The other part of the bookends that bound my childhood life was the Erb Street Mennonite Church. In those days the Old Mennonites,

Both these paintings, Humble Beginnings *(above) and* Waterloo Market *(below) are scenes from the neighbourhood in which I was raised.*

It seemed to me as a child that the rhythm of school and church was interrupted only by Summer Bible School. It is fun to look back at a picture such as this. I am the kid extreme right.

as we were called, had quite definite rules. There was to be no drinking, dancing or smoking. Women were pressed not to cut their hair or wear jewellery or makeup. No one went to movie theatres. That sort of stricture has now relaxed, I'm told. Marilyn and I are no longer practising Mennonites. My brother, Doug, who works for me, is a lay minister for that church. He spends much time visiting hospitals and nursing homes. I commend him. As a child I attended church twice on Sunday, morning and evening, and also Wednesday evening. To say that this regime was too confining shows that I have a keen grasp of the obvious. In later years as a teenager, Friday night Mennonite Youth Fellowship also became part of the drill. That night was much less negative. If I didn't watch myself, I actually enjoyed it. By the teenage years I was dispatched to Rockway Mennonite High School. There, too, the barriers were tight. Out of those years, however, some good things emerged. It was there I met my bride of thirty years, Marilyn. I also made some very long term friends. Thankfully at this point I was starting painting lessons which, it turns out, remains my passion.

This is the print cut from the Star Weekly *that hung over the piano at home. I think I spent more time looking at the picture than practising the piano.*

As a shy, fat twelve year old, our family's move from the downtown neighbourhood out to the suburbs was traumatic. Because I finished my year at my old school, I had a period of about six months where I did not know any of the kids in my new neighbourhood. Although it was painful at the time, I realize now that those months gave me a window where all my spare time was spent painting. With that kind of time plus Saturday afternoon lessons for ten weeks with Cole Bowman, I was able to develop my painting quite a bit.

When I finally got to my new school I had developed a bit of a profile as an artist. Let's face it, in grade eight it takes very little. I received a little extra attention because of this. It was very confirming for me.

Although my four years of high school at Rockway contained no formal art instruction from the school, at the age of fifteen, along with my mother I was privileged to join a Saturday class at M. F. Kousal's studio. Because I was so keen to learn, I progressed quickly. It was the right thing at the right time. Matt Kousal held classes in his second floor studio/gallery. He hosted about sixteen students at a time. Those two hours were, for me, the shortest hours of the week. On a potbellied stove, a branch of pine stood in a can of warm water. The smell of oil paints mixed with the pine aroma to create a bouquet that I still recall vividly. Beyond the painting devices that I learned from him was an idea that directed the course of my life. I saw that this Czech immigrant was able to make a living as an artist. He was the first real artist I got to know. A picture of his that we cut from the *Star Weekly* used to hang over our piano. I was so inspired as I saw what went into the art that he made. His appealing style of painting absorbed into my pores. While at Kousal's lessons I met another young would-be artist, Mike Roth. Although we met and chatted at this time, it was not until six or eight years later that we became fast friends. After my disastrous show of paintings of Europe, I teamed up with Mike. For several years we shared a studio and tried to figure life in an attempt to stay alive as artists. To this day, every Thursday that both Mike and I are in town we get together for lunch. We are still trying to figure out what making a living as an artist means. During this time I was prowling the Kitchener Public Library sussing out books on painting. This time was long before all the current how-to books produced by professional artists. The library did contain bound copies of two British magazines *The Artist* and *Studio*. Already at this point I was drawing to me strong influences that would affect my life and painting.

This is my version of a painting by M.F. Kousal. I painted it in 1961.

This painting, Gathering At The Meeting House, *has become a signature image for me. I sometimes wish that I could make some changes but if I start, I will never finish.*

When I was seventeen I decided to visit a horse and buggy church with my friends John and Leroy. With the aid of a calendar provided by the Old Order Church, we were able to determine where the service would be that particular Sunday. Services, you see, rotate from building to building. The small distances travelled comfortably by horse make this rotation necessary. When the horse and buggy people use Meeting House A, the black bumper or Waterloo Markham people meet at Church B. These black bumper people, so called because they used to paint all the chrome on their cars black, are a split-off from the Old Order Mennonite (horse and buggy) Church. This alternating system assures a well-used building.

Since this Sunday visit was thirty-seven years ago, my memory of the service is quite general. The entire service was conducted in Pennsylvania Deutsch, a Low German dialect. I was in deep trouble. I did not speak Low German, much to the chagrin of my grandmother Snyder. "I don't see why Mommy didn't learn you the German" she'd say. The reason was, of course, that following the war it was not too cool to speak German, and my mother, ever conscious of what people thought, made a distinct decision to not teach us Deutsch. She and my father kept it as their private language. I have certainly wished over my thirty years of dealing with the Old Order Mennonites that I could have handled their language. Typical of any ethnic group, their exclusive language is an invisible dividing line between them and outsiders.

When I first displayed this painting at the Provident Book Store, a little conservative Mennonite lady told me that this painting was all inclusive. She said, "It contains life, death and worship. Even the out-houses behind the church 'convey the daily round, the common task, will furnish all we ought to ask'." People often add their own point of view to my paintings. Those responses extend the paintings and are always interesting to me. Often those new thoughts bring on more paintings.

There is, for me, great excitement at a Mennonite church as the people pour out after service. For a few moments this view becomes as congested as any city street scene that I could want to paint. Then slowly, bit by bit, the energy dissipates and the tranquility of the plain wooden building returns.

The only relief from Pennsylvania Deutsch at this typical service was bible reading and singing in High German. It strikes me as an irony today that at that point in my life I would have been more at home in French, from my studies, or even Latin. Strange, isn't it, that at Rockway, a Mennonite High School, there were courses in French and Latin but none in Pennsylvania Deutsch, our traditional tongue.

After almost three hours of unintelligible sermons and several sessions of prayer as well as Gregorian Chant-type singing, we were mercifully released. At the time I was not really aware of it but I am sure our presence ran a very strong competition to the worship service. The fun, however, was just to begin. As we filed out no one greeted us or made any welcoming signs. It was only after the bishop came and talked to us that we were deemed fit for conversation. I have noticed this strong group control again and again as, over the last thirty years, I have seen the appropriate authority either make or break a farm visit. If the father or grandfather decides that I am acceptable then other members of the family are willing to chat. But only if their family leader shows the way.

We, the three musketeers, were invited to dinner at one of the farms close by. We found the farm quite easily. Driving by this farm over the last thirty years I have not stopped to renew acquaintances. I should have but I was just too shy and I guess afraid that without the proper stamp of approval I would not be welcome. I am sure I do these people a disservice.

After mountains of food, the three of us retreated to the comfort zone of our car. It seems strange to me that one of the strongest memories that I have of that dinner is a two year old girl. Much was made of her as she had been in some awful accident and our hosts were sure that we would remember it was in the newspaper. Although I had always known, this church visit and the subsequent dinner showed me just how narrow and confining that traditional Mennonite life is. It did not suit me and yet somehow I am drawn to it. Why?

ONTARIO COLLEGE OF ART

When I entered Ontario College of Art in the fall of 1963, the group that I joined was a gathering of outstanding art students from high schools across Ontario. In those days, the two real art colleges in Canada were Ontario College of Art in Toronto and the Ecole des Beaux Arts in Montreal. This was long before the rise of community colleges. It seems strange now when competition to enter specialty programs is so intense that during those times it was easy to get in. Without a high school art portfolio I had little to show but was accepted anyway. Because I was lacking in confidence about my background education, I decided to take a History of Art course that summer at Carleton University. I was hoping it would give me some information and some confidence. What I did not expect was my first contact with a commercial art gallery. After I finished my first class at Carleton, I decided to go downtown to explore a bit. I discovered an art gallery right in the middle of Sparks Street pedestrian mall. It occurred to me that perhaps I could sell some paintings to help me defer my art college expenses. I telephoned home and requested that my mom send a few of my finished paintings up to Ottawa. I had taken my painting gear along to Carleton but what I needed were a few examples of my completed work. When I showed these paintings to the owner of the gallery, Bruce Hay, he quite readily agreed to give my things a try. In the next several days there was enough interest on the part of the public that Bruce decided that I should paint on the street. Looking back on it now, I realize that this four-week period in Ottawa gave me my first public contact, my first real dealer, my first chance to fly as picture-maker and, oh yeah, I also learned something of the history of art.

Part of my art college education was a week each year spent drawing at the Royal Winter Fair. Great fun and, for me, rather prophetic.

The curriculum at art college was a four year process. The first year all the students took a variety of courses to provide an insight into many areas of art. Ranging from two and three dimensional design through watercolour painting, figure painting, sculpture, colour theory, weaving, lettering and art history, these courses helped students to select the area of specialization for the following three years. Although I flirted briefly with the idea of sculpture as a specialty, I decided on Drawing and Painting, as the course was then called. When shortened to D & P, it is not difficult to see how our specialty became deviants and perverts to the other students. I think that I was very fortunate to have been at college when many of the instructors still had personal contact with some of the Group of Seven. Although the Group of Seven was avant-garde in its time, it seemed quite traditional in 1963. I especially enjoyed my contact with the older instructors because of their more traditional, technique-oriented approach. There was another group of instructors that were much more abstract in their painting style and made strong efforts to influence the students in that direction. My marks with both groups were very ordinary. I was showing no personal style and, I am afraid, not much progress until third year. It would seem that for me, the penny dropped relative to drawing and its application to painting at the start of that year. Following years one and two, I had spent the summers flogging my paintings on the street in Ottawa and Stratford. The painting that I was doing was of the Matt Kousal style, northern Ontario landscape. These modest paintings sold for appropriately modest prices - fifteen to seventy dollars. Those summer sessions did several things for me. First, they supplied money for the following year's tuition and room. Second, I got to deal with the public and perform in public. The public, as I soon learned, is as nice or nasty as the individual involved. I had people tell me to my face that what I did was crap and others told me with money how much they liked what I did.

Pencil crayon drawing from the Royal Winter Fair during my third year at O.C.A.

I remember in particular an older woman who looked at my paintings in the glass cases on the Sparks Street Mall and decided that she must have three of them. The financial transaction was done but how was she to get them home? Since she did not drive and went everywhere by bus, she had a brief quandary. After a few minutes in Woolworths, she emerged with a package of washline rope. Lashing her paintings quickly together, she disappeared onto the bus as I stood there with my mouth open.

The third year at college was a bit tricky for me. On one hand, I had turned the corner technically while on the other I found myself at loggerheads with the more avant-garde instructors. There was a real tension within the department with the two warring groups of instructors recruiting for their team. My conservative position was further highlighted as I started to include a few Mennonite motifs in my work. Even for the conservative group my Mennonite work was questionable; to the less structured group my Mennonite work was unfathomable. I found myself in a difficult situation. I had never felt totally comfortable in Toronto although I was fortunate to live for several years with a high school friend who worked at the Bank of Montreal. Together with my future brother-in-law and my cousin, as well as a number of Kitchener-Waterloo people we formed a society within a society. Every weekend I would get a lift with either Don or Bruce back to Waterloo. This gave me a chance to see Marilyn, who later became my wife, to teach art in my parents' basement and to reconnect with Mennonite country.

As my third year progressed the differences that I had with certain instructors escalated. You can imagine my chagrin when at the end of third year a major shake-up was announced in the teaching staff. The avant-garde group had won and the conservatives were fired. Obviously, from my standpoint, they had trashed the wrong group. Their decision sealed my decision not to return for fourth year. Dropping out of art college was not startling. Indeed, of the thirty-some students who had started second year in drawing and painting, only three graduated. I was not one of them.

This painting speaks strongly about how I felt about our first crossing of the Atlantic on the 10,000 ton Franconia.

Christmas of 1966 found Marilyn and I in a down-at-the-heels guesthouse in Vienna. We had discovered this backstreet hotel in Arthur Frommer's *Europe On $5.00 A Day*. That kind of a price range was necessary as we had planned to stay in Europe for a year. Following our wedding in September my father had very calmly written us a cheque for $4500. He reasoned that he had paid that for each of my brothers to go to college so an equal amount in my direction would be fair. Since I had already paid for my three years at O.C.A. by teaching art and selling my paintings, this money from Dad was manna from heaven. Marilyn and I had persuaded her brother Don and his new wife, also Marilyn, that a year in Europe would be ideal. We could get jobs as necessary or so we thought. In October we sailed on the 10,000 ton *Franconia*. Marilyn's diary reveals that I was only really sick for twenty-four hours; I remember a much worse crossing. Travelling from Holland to Spain, from France to Vienna, gave me a wonderful

Both these paintings, Green Umbrellas *(above) and* Barcelona Houses,
resulted from my first encounter with the Mediterranian landscape.

NEAR ALICENTE
SOUTH-EAST COAST
OF SPAIN

Both these drawings were done on our first trip to Europe.
Although I did quite a few things during those three months,
not very many survive. I am sorry now that I was not more
careful but organization and neatness have never been my
strong suits. Even back then I was more interested in the doing
of paintings than the keeping of them. When we returned home
I did many drawings in pencil or charcoal that should have had
fixative applied to prevent smudging. Unfortunately, I am a
slow learner. It took me quite a few years to realize that I did
not have an endless supply of drawings within me. (Upper left)
Baden-Baden, (lower left) east coast of Spain.

chance to compare the real thing with the images that I had in my
mind from the study of European art. We fatefully finished our
trip in England. In January London does not show its best face but
that face was plenty good enough for us. We certainly did not
expect that our life would allow us to go back to that sceptered isle
over twenty times in the next thirty years. Browsing through
London used-book shops I came upon the work of two artists that
I admire to this day. The first was Edward Seago. I had chanced
upon his work in Toronto during my art college days. I had been
infected by his romantic scenes at a show at the Laing Gallery. The
other artist that froze me in my tracks was Sir Alfred Munnings,
P.R.A. This painter of equestrian portraits and describer of gypsy
life in Britain suggested an idea that echoed in my mind of
Mennonite life at home. Although I never got to meet either of
these painters, they changed my life. Along with these two, another
artist that has influenced my painting is artist/illustrator, Terrence
Cuneo. Art College had prepared the ground but these three artists
provided the seed for my artistic life. I was so fortunate in 1995 to
actually meet Terrence Cuneo at his studio near London. I took
him my book *A Painter's Harvest*. Later, I received from him a
carefully considered letter in which he talked about individual
pictures in it. I treasure it.
After three months it was good to get back from Europe with so
many new impressions.

Marilyn took a job at the Kitchener Public Library fairly soon after our return from our honeymoon. It was a good thing as I was not having very good luck at selling my paintings. From my studio above a shoe store in downtown Waterloo, I had mounted a show of paintings that I did upon our return from Europe. I wrongly assumed that the public would be as enthused about Europe as I was. This disastrous show was held at the Provident Bookstore in Kitchener. While in art school I had been fortunate enough to hold a fairly successful exhibition at this store; however, the European show died. I sold nothing. I had foolishly spent a largish amount of money to frame these pieces as I had hoped to make a splash. I did. Unfortunately it was a belly-flop. Money was extremely tight for us in those days and we survived only because our third floor King Street apartment was so cheap ($45 a month). My studio was also a less than prime location and the rent reflected that fact. For the first few months after our return from Europe we had no car

This photo from the K-W Record in 1966 demonstrates my situation as I am just getting serious about the Mennonite theme. The photo was taken outside the blacksmith shop in St. Jacobs.

but got around on the Honda 55cc bike I had used in Art College. Although I had taught briefly at Doon School of Fine Arts, where the kids named me Supersketch, I decided to teach privately at my studio. The fall-back of all painters seems to be teaching and that is exactly how I tried to raise some funds. My studio was roomy enough although it was difficult to persuade students to lug their painting boxes up the incredibly high Victorian staircase. Even with private students, my income was pitiful and so I decided to do some public painting as a way of attracting attention and sales. Once again the good merchants of K-W helped me out. I made a deal with Beaupre's paint and paper store to paint for several weekends in their window. I did manage to sell two paintings at the princely sums of $80 and $85. One Saturday morning Mike Roth, whom I had met at Matt Kousal's in my teen years, came to Beaupre's. Since he had quit his job to try his luck full-time as an artist we had much in common. After a lot of discussion we decided to try a joint assault on our careers. Mike joined me in my studio and we put together a group of paintings that we hoped we might sell in shopping malls. We had, of course, no idea which shopping malls. I should note that there were very few. The malling of North America was just starting. We decided that we should go to the United States. On a snowy January morning we drove to Buffalo, N.Y. in the worst weather I have ever seen. Any reasonable person would have stayed home but such was our head of steam that we plowed on. A border crossing guard suggested a mall that we could try. Through dumb luck we found the mall manager in and receptive. A date was made for a show a few months in the future and we were launched. For two months we worked feverishly to add to the meagre stock of paintings that we already owned. Since we had thirty days to pay for picture frames we arranged a very large order for a week before the show date in Buffalo. With the clock running for payment we set up our exhibit in the mall. To our pleasant surprise, our Northern Ontario landscapes were a modest success. People at the mall identified with our images as views from their cottages, either in Ontario or the Adirondacks. Elated, we arranged to extend our stay at the mall. That show led to numbers of others over the next eighteen months. We even hired two more people to help us. We would paint for several months and then do a mall show. Sometimes our helpers staffed the shows.

Although this small success was intoxicating, I began to realize that I did not want to spend my life as an itinerant painter. Marilyn and I decided if I was going to have a chance to paint Waterloo County I'd best get started. We concluded that to get established we needed our own gallery. We started the depressing task of trying to find a house that was both within our budget and properly zoned. After many forays our agent, Ford, sold us the house on Erb Street that is our gallery today. For a number of years we lived on the main floor while renting out the second floor apartment. My studio/gallery was in the basement. I started once again to teach private classes in oil painting. It was a nip and tuck existence made possible by two things - our tenant's rent and Marilyn's pay cheque. Then several pieces of good fortune came along. Ford, our real estate agent, mentioned to his mother that he had sold a house to a fellow who intended to specialize in paintings of Waterloo County. His mother, Nora Milhausen, was interested because one of her tasks as a member of the board of the Kitchener-Waterloo Hospital was the purchase of art for the new hospital addition. She came, she saw, she bought. The purchase of fifteen paintings was monumental to me. It confirmed that, yes, someone else was interested in my work. Nora also consented to

Edna Staebler, who has since become a friend, was on the board of the Kitchener Public Library when Marilyn worked there in the children's department. This portrait of Edna and her cats hangs in that institution.

host an exhibition of my paintings in our living room the following year. Since she was a long-time member of the Westmount Golf Club her mailing list included most of the social cream of the twin cities. The living room/dining room show was a success. This was the first pebble in the pond.

Close to that time one of the students from my subterranean classes asked if I knew who might evaluate a painting that she and her husband had just recently inherited. Jean Hart, bless her soul, by that question put another drama in place for me. I suggested that the director of Eaton's College Street Gallery in Toronto would certainly be able to identify a Krieghoff and that, if he did come, would she please, please, please send him over to see me and my work. He came, he saw, he liked. Yes, I could show my work on a trial basis at Eaton's Art Gallery on College Street in Toronto. During those years of the early seventies many well-off people from across Ontario purchased paintings from that well-known gallery. My work was well received by the public and I was launched outside of Waterloo County.

For several years I taught in the basement of our home on Erb Street. I am pleased that the young woman shown here with me, Chris Baker Hallman, now owns an art gallery/framing shop. P.S. I was in my Elvis mode at the time.

Unknown to me, one of the purchasers was Keith MacDonald, the president of Industrial Acceptance Corp. Also unknown to me, Mr. MacDonald had known my father and uncle when they were starting in the dairy business on a farm just north of Waterloo. At that point he was a school teacher boarding at a farm next to Maple Lane Dairy.

Mr. MacDonald decided to reproduce one of my paintings for their company's Christmas card but, through an oversight, no one got my copyright approval. Only after the card was printed and sent was the mistake uncovered. One day I got a call from my dad that he had received a letter at Maple Lane Dairy from Mr. MacDonald. Because of my middle name, he had correctly assumed that I was Etril's son. The letter asked how much I wanted for the reproduction rights. I phoned Mr. MacDonald and said that I was thrilled to have had one of my things reproduced for a big company like theirs and did not wish any compensation. He then kindly invited me to Toronto to their luxurious head office and

This is the first full colour published work of mine. It was used by I.A.C. Ltd. as their Christmas card in 1973.

This traditional Mennonite farmhouse near Kaufman's Flats still stands even though over twenty years ago I thought that it was doomed by development.

asked me to bring some paintings with me. At this meeting he purchased all six of the paintings I brought along. I was thrilled almost to tears. This was my first experience selling to a corporation. It started me down a road that has led to many corporate customers.

During the early and middle 1970's, I continued to show my work at Eaton's Art Gallery on College Street in Toronto and at a few other small art dealers around the greater Toronto area. Any spare money we got helped finance another trip to England. By this point we were well and truly hooked on the U.K. Unfortunately, management changes at Eaton's Art Gallery were starting to bring me difficulties. As a new director of the gallery came in from Montreal, he brought with him artists whose work he knew from that city. This gave me my first indication that I may have to present my own work instead of relying on a dealer. About this time too, I had a few of the smaller dealers "forget" to pay me for paintings that they had sold. Marilyn and I decided to take over the whole house on Erb Street so that we could open a by-appointment gallery. Now, as well as living on the ground floor we had a bedroom upstairs plus a gallery and my studio space. The arrangement worked quite well and I was glad for our changes when Eaton's Art Gallery on College Street was severely limited by the move into the new Eaton's Centre in downtown Toronto. Through these years, however, we continued with Neales, a small jewellery shop in Tillsonburg which housed a constant show of paintings by Mike Roth and me. I learned that a small town can service a large area. Ironically, not once did I have any problems with this Tillsonburg arrangement while the big city dealers needed constant watching.

Through the middle 70's my prices started to escalate simply because I was having problems keeping up to the demand from the public. This was a surprise. When I first started with my Mennonite subjects, local people would suggest that these farm paintings were of very little interest. "Why don't you paint the Rockies or something?" Well it seemed to me then, as it seems to me now, that those farm paintings, those views of Mennonite country were charming. The name Mennonite country came from the title of a book which teamed my black and white drawings with text by an Old Order Amish farmer. In discussions with Paul and Hildi Tiessen, the publishers, the Mennonite country term emerged and became the title of that now out-of-print book.

In 1976 we decided to take the plunge. We opened our own gallery and started publishing limited edition reproductions. On our continuing trips to England we had seen the limited edition idea gathering strength. What a practical way to present artwork to the public at a reasonable price. We had, since 1969, been vendors at the Kitchener Market where Marilyn and later my sister-in-law, Katherine, sold our small open edition black and white reproductions. Now, for our new gallery/shop, we had black and white prints and cards, hand-tinted versions of those black and whites and, starting nervously, a few full colour limited edition reproductions.

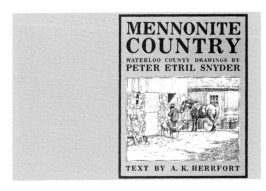

Published by Sand Hills Books, Inc., this volume teamed the writings of an Old Order Amish farmer with my ink drawings. It was a pleasure to work with the publisher who is a friend from high school days.

This set of four reproductions (18"x24") marked our start at colour reproduction work.

Although Marilyn and I had been to England and Europe several times before 1976 it was in that year that we increased our travel. By this point we were organized enough at the gallery/shop that it was not necessary for me to be there daily. We developed the idea that it was my job to get the paintings onto the walls and it was the job of staff to get them off — to sell them. This was our first winter in Florida. Although it took us until 1991 to find Key West as our winter base, the die of southern winters was cast. I had already done a good deal of painting when we travelled. Now, in Florida, I found calm. I could really throw myself into painting. Using photo files that I brought from home I constructed compositions.

From photos that I took, as well as photos from Williamsburg
archives, I developed a set of four paintings including
Mid-Morning, Duke of Gloucester Street *(shown above).*

On our way back from Florida we visited Williamsburg, Virginia. The connection was immediate. When the summer came, we visited France and England again. That trip gave us our first taste of Sissinghurst, that extra ordinary garden in Kent. It also was our first visit to Rye, Sussex down on the south coast. It was there, in that pretty walled town, that we rented a house, Oak Corner, some years later.

This painting looking out from the churchyard was just one of many that I produced during our second visit to Rye, Sussex in 1979.

These four paintings were done during my time as artist-in-residence at Conrad Grebel College. I have since held that position at a number of institutions.

Looking back on this year I realize how busy we had become. That was the year that we did major renovations to our house to make it into a true house/gallery combination. As all this activity continued, I kept working as if the paintings needed to escape from within me. I had always been a morning person and realized that for me, the morning was the time to paint. I have never been able to identify with stories of artists who paint right through the night. I find that if I paint for four hours in a day I am totally drained of energy. If I paint longer I get overly tired and am unable to make any painting progress the next day. That lack of progress makes me very frustrated.

Stylistically I was developing quite strongly through the late seventies. I learned how to better focus my point of view. This may have been helped by travels to France and England. During that time we also went to Washington, D.C. and New York City to visit

Even though I am best known for country subjects, I also love painting street scenes such as this one in New York City. I have done street paintings from Paris to Mexico City. My concern is always, "What is light doing to the subject?"

public galleries both to see their permanent collections and special shows.

No story of my life can be told without the mention of a journey to England in 1977 for the Queen's Jubilee. We arrived from France where we had toured the Loire valley. Our English stay started at the Miller Howe Hotel in the Lake District. This dramatic hotel is run by a former actor who operates his hostelry as a stage. We were treated to a replica of the coronation dinner accompanied by harp and lute music. What fun to see a man run his hotel as performance art.

My father was a very quiet man who was interested in things that were practical. Although he never sought to hold me back in my career, he certainly did not understand why I would wish to pursue painting.

That trip was notable, too, for a drama that we witnessed from the White Hart Hotel in Lincoln. On the eve of our Queen's Jubilee, Her Majesty lit a signal fire in Windsor Great Park. When that light was sighted another bonfire was lit on a hill some distance away. That firelight signalled to another hill. They lit their fire. This progress of illumination spread across the land as we watched it on television. What a thrill it was to look from our third story window to see the beacon lit on a hill outside the city and to watch that fire appear on our television screen. Jubilee year was extra special for Marilyn and I because we met my father in London and had several days of good crack, as the Irish say. He had always wanted to go to England and here he was with us in that celebratory year.

On our almost yearly trips to the U.K. I made it a habit to stop in at Ontario House in London. It is through that location that Ontario and all its wonderful attributes are represented to the British public. On one occasion in 1978 I happened to be in the office of their publicity person when the then-Agent General, Ward Cornell of hockey fame, stopped by. When he heard I was from Kitchener-Waterloo we talked a bit about the Mennonites and how I paint their lifestyle. He was quite intrigued by the brochure of my work. When he had lived in London, Ontario, he regularly visited the Kitchener Market to buy items from some of the Mennonite vendors. He wondered if I would be interested in displaying my work at Ontario House. I was delighted as I hoped to perhaps attract some British attention to my work. Although the gallery was really a large general purpose room in the basement of the building, it was well lighted and appropriate for an exhibition. Using the Ontario House mailing list, we had a good turnout of people for the four-day show. We were fortunate enough to have some aristocracy attend as well. It was at that show that I met Paul Martin, Sr., Canadian High Commissioner to the Court of St. James. Mr. Martin invited Marilyn and me to cocktails at the official residence in Upper Brook Street where he commissioned me to do his portrait. For a young artist the London show along with the portrait commission was heady stuff. Once again my good luck held.

(Left) Overview of show. (Above) Marilyn talking with Lord and Lady McFadzean. (Below) Working on the portrait of Paul Martin, Sr. at our house in Rye, Sussex.

Sometimes it is difficult to erase an idea from your mind. In 1979 a most pleasant fellow came to my studio/gallery suggesting that I should do some plate designs for a company that he was starting. Horst Mueller was charming and certainly most knowledgeable about porcelain, having trained as a porcelain-maker in Germany. However, stuck in my mind was a vision of white and blue Danish plates. He returned with some magazines showing full colour collector plates which were just coming to the market. I was flattered that he felt my paintings could provide viable designs for a new venture but I was still sceptical about the whole collector plate idea and of the technology needed to reproduce my colours.

Although twelve designs were selected for the Preserving A Way Of Life series, I did produce many other round designs. For a brief time we talked about Horses Around The World and shown above are three of those preliminary sketches. Perhaps in the future this idea will be revisited.

As we talked, an idea emerged that would allow a cautious entry into the field. Christian Bell Porcelain, Horst's company, could produce four images to start; one from each season. If this beginning found success we would follow with another set of four to be rounded off with the third set of four, giving us one design for each month of the year. Horst's connection with both the chinamen, as we called the porcelain manufacturers, and the retail trade proved invaluable. For many years he had represented some of the top European porcelain-makers to china stores in Ontario. At the very first plate/trade show the entire first set or chapter, as we came to call it, was fully subscribed. In the several years following that launch, I travelled across the province and even across Canada appearing at collectables' shows and dealers. Once again my experience of painting in public, first tried in my student years, proved invaluable. I painted and signed, signed and painted. I visited with thousands of people as I represented my designs. This exposure also introduced many people to my limited edition reproductions and stimulated a whole new group to collect my work. Once again someone had come into my life from stage left and introduced me to a whole new audience.

By 1979 it was becoming apparent that if Marilyn and I wished to continue to travel and if I was to get any painting accomplished, it would be necessary to have more help. We had already hired two women to staff the shop but we needed some management help. In typical Mennonite style I turned to my brother Doug.

We realized that we would feel comfortable only with someone who understood us and the Mennonite subject. Doug was ideally suited. For nine years Doug had worked for the Mennonite Central Committee which, I realize, sounds like some Communist organization. It is, however, the relief and service arm of the Mennonite Church. In that position he had represented several of the horse and buggy Mennonite groups in dealings with the government. These contacts provided an excellent education for him into the whys and wherefores of the conservative Mennonite and Amish groups. It was so fortuitous that he was ready for a change of job just at a time when we needed some informed help. Once again fortune smiled on me.

Brother Doug, shown above, has provided me a consistent steadying hand for almost twenty years. His day-to-day efforts make our frequent travel possible.

Mr. & Mrs. Schickedanz from Toronto were buyers of two of the fourteen paintings offered at a price-establishing auction we held in 1979. I have been very fortunate that many people like Mr. & Mrs. Schickedanz have continuously collected my work over many years. Many collectors have become more than purchasers, they have become friends.

Because I was unsure of what to charge I did not sell the fourteen original paintings we had reproduced as limited editions. As time went on and the requests to purchase those originals increased, I felt the only way to establish a price for reproduced works would be through auction. This was very traumatic for me since my future seemed on the line. I have a tendency to over-react to tense situations with nervous energy. The auction that was held at the Waterloo Motor Inn indicated that the public valued the published works at approximately twice the price of a comparable unreproduced painting. That Sunday afternoon in 1979 was a remarkable day for me. Besides netting around $80,000, it also set a framework for future endeavours. It also made me sick for several days as the nervous energy dissipated.

In 1980 we first visited Bermuda. We had seen photos of this crescent of islands and they suggested a southern version of England. Our connection to the Windjammer gallery was made through the kind help of Bob Furey, a friend from Rotary. Our personal connection to the people at the gallery was immediate. Since that time we have visited Bermuda several times. Once we rented a house for a month. How fortunate for us that we can go to a new country and have not only a business connection but also a social circle.

This commissioned painting for a Bermuda resident shows a view very near the home of my Bermuda dealer. We had the good fortune while working on this piece to receive an invitation to Easter Breakfast at my dealers' home. A beautiful brunch featuring the traditional cod cakes was followed by several hours of kite flying from her cliff top home.

This photo from 1983 shows me in my gallery surrounded by my paintings and my sculpture. Over the years I have hired photographers to take series of shots to be used by newspapers and magazines. This is one of those publicity shots.

While in art college I had taken several courses in sculpture and found that I was reasonably good at three dimensional modelling. I decided to try my hand at cold cast bronze as the collector plates had put me in touch with many gift shops. I modelled (in plasticine) four figures that were cast in Warkworth, Ontario by Chris Gosset. Chris is now best known for his wildlife bird sculptures in cold cast bronze. Since he was just starting, he agreed to cast my pieces in a mixture of bronze powder and acrylic known as cold cast bronze. For several years that project was quite successful and was terminated only by Chris's move to British Columbia.

43

This painting hangs in the foyer at the Grand River Conservation Authority. This large (3'x4') painting was unveiled by Lord Baden-Powell.

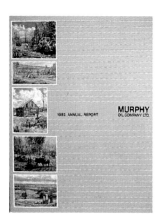

I had the good fortune to create a group of paintings for Murphy Oil Company Ltd. which they used in their annual report. I was flown by them around Alberta and parts of Saskatchewan to see their operations. After having those photos developed at a one hour photo shop, I had the evening to develop sketches for presentation to their President the next morning. Fortunately, he approved. It helped that he himself is an amateur artist.

In 1985 I started my continuing relationship with the Grand River Conservation Foundation. My first work for them was a large acrylic entitled *Downstream*. That piece was followed by a series of black and white drawings that appeared weekly in newspapers along the watershed. My latest effort for conservation was a set of train paintings. Reproductions of those three works have been used to raise money for the Rails To Trails endeavour. This project has involved purchasing unused railway rights of way and converting them for recreational walking or biking. I personally hope that with time this idea can be expanded to include comfort stations and pubs along the way. Marilyn and I have spent many happy hours on walking trails in the U.K. from pub to pub. Another conservation connection for me was the presentation of one of my paintings, *The Homestead*, to H.R.H. Prince Philip as he inaugurated Rocky Mountain Park in Alberta. I was not present when The Hon. Joe Clark made the presentation but I was fortunate to meet Prince Philip at the Royal Winter Fair (photo below) in 1996. We had a pleasant chat about my work and the paintings of a British artist that we both admire, Edward Seago.

I am very surprised at the number of important people in business and public life that are keen amateur painters. Prince Philip is one of these. I wonder if the desire to make something new in paint is an extension of their creative professional lives.

In 1989 I had the good fortune to receive commissions from two divisions of the Upjohn Company. While the pharmaceutical division requested The Doctor's Return *(shown above)*, the animal health care division wanted an image incorporating a newly-born animal. Strangely, neither division realized that I was doing a painting for the other. It's a funny old world!

This painting was commissioned to preserve the idea of this family home near Oshawa. This farm is now, I suppose, covered with a subdivision.

After her training in textiles Marilyn decided that tapestry weaving was not really what she wished to pursue. It would seem to me that gardening has taken over as her main artistic pursuit.

A Painter's Harvest
The Works of Peter Etril Snyder

I co-published this book with C.B.C. Enterprises. As is typical of the way I work, I totally developed the book right down to colour separations before I went looking for a publisher.

A lottery to select models for this painting helped raise funds for the Juvenile Diabetes Foundation. The Foundation also sold reproductions as well as the original to make this a very successful project.

For several years we were fortunate to present our annual exhibition at the Seagram Museum in Waterloo (above). Over the years we have presented our annual show either at a hotel or our own gallery. Shows like this give me a chance to show a group of new works together which, I think, gives greater impact.

This painting was a unique opportunity to picture an animal that had a major impact in the quarter-horse business. Part of the challenge was to capture the unusual way that this horse held his head. Although Show Tip is no longer alive I hear quite often of his progeny and their show results.

It would be wrong to say that Marilyn and I are fans of the opera. To paraphrase the song ... I'm a little bit country, she's a little bit rock 'n roll. It was, however, an exciting time when a friend from our teen-age years debuted at the Metropolitan Opera in New York. Paul Frey, a former truck driver from St. Jacobs, has gone far and achieved much. We were pleased to see him in *Ariade auf Naxos* at Lincoln Centre in New York. We had dinner the next evening at the Café des Artistes because we knew Linda and Paul, who live in Switzerland, would enjoy this romantic restaurant.

It was this gathering place, with its mirror-reflected murals that inspired our contribution to Janet Lynn's Bistro in Waterloo. Although the subject matter for my murals is quite different from the wood nymphs of Howard Chandler Christy's, the placement of the murals with the mirrored walls is directly related.

How pleasant it is when a customer proposes a commission painting of an area that we have visited and loved. On our twenty-fifth anniversary in 1991 we had enjoyed the sweeping views of the Irish coast. This painting was created to commemorate the fiftieth birthday of our customer's wife. Quite a surprise.

Companies often mark their anniversaries by commissioning a painting of their beginnings as was the case for Shur-Gain (left) and Erb Transport (right).

Even while developing commission works for individuals and corporations I continued to explore the landscape of Waterloo County. I found that often through commissioned works I was introduced to visual ideas that also occurred in Mennonite country. A different effect of light or composition can trigger a new line of inquiry and force me to re-examine what I thought was a familiar view.

In 1989 I received a dream commission from National Trust to paint a boardroom mural that showed scenes across Canada. After travelling our country and taking thousands of photos, I painted the 5'x15' mural in public. Although most of my ideas for this work came from our trip and consultations with the president of the company, the public also helped me to decide what to leave out and what to include. I also created nineteen paintings for other parts of National Trust's new headquarters on Yonge Street in Toronto. All of the work attempted to show the variety of people, industry and geography across Canada. Perhaps an opportunity like this comes along only once in a lifetime. I hope not.

Although I had worked on the paintings for eighteen months, the mural was installed just one day before the grand opening (right).

Our English travels over the following several years focused to a large degree on the Cotswolds. That area near Stratford and Bath is so pretty and so made for painting with its buff coloured stone cottages and colourful gardens. It was during 1989 that I placed paintings with an art dealer in Broadway, John Noott 20th Century Ltd. This gallery is close to Buckland Manor, a hotel that we particularly admire. We had our twenty-fifth wedding celebration there - lunch with my brothers and their wives. Marilyn and I had joined them for their twenty-fifth wedding celebrations just two years earlier at this same hotel (photo above). I suppose that it says something about the way we think that our travel here and abroad is linked to hotels, restaurants and pubs that hold an emotional appeal for us.

Sue Dobson, the editor of Woman and Home *magazine became aware of my work in 1977 through Ontario House in London, England. Our friendship has grown over the years and she has featured my work four times in her magazine.*

We had a dark spot in our life in 1989. My sister-in-law Doreen became deathly ill with a lung condition. One lung was totally non-functioning while the second was operating on only a small percentage of normal capacity. On December 2nd she had a single lung transplant in London, Ontario. The operation proved successful but the road to recovery, such as it is, was a long and difficult one. She now leads an almost normal life although in a somewhat careful way. I remark on this because other than my father's quick death of cancer in 1983 my life has been charmed and I realize it.

A commission to create a painting to commemorate the centennial of the Presbyterian church at Doon gave me a chance to use my niece and her new husband as models (photo above). As often as possible I like to use friends and family to guide me as I develop a painting. I have found it useful to have a session with a professional photographer so that I am free to direct the poses rather than trying to take the pictures myself.

Near the end of the eighties I had the fun of painting with a group of artists one night a week in a factory/studio. We hired models, both nude and costumed. Not since my college days had I worked with so keen a group of painters. It was fun. Marilyn and I called it the Naked Lady Painting Group.

The presentation of my painting at Royal Canadian Mounted Police Headquarters was exciting and satisfying for me. The whole Mountie experience rekindled my boyhood joy in the musical ride and horses in general. How clearly I remember my father driving up to our house with the milk wagon. While he had his lunch the horse stood patiently munching away from his oats bag. My dad would attach a rope that had a thirty pound weight to the horse's halter. I was allowed to go out and play with the horse and climb around inside the wagon.

My affection for horses is obvious in my work. I was pleased to receive my only equestrian portrait commission from GEC Alsthom. They wished to honour their retiring president who hails from France. We travelled to his farm in the Eastern Townships of Quebec to see this accomplished man with his horse. I was pleased with the result and received a letter from him saying how much he enjoyed the painting and that it hangs at his retirement home on the Riviera.

While I was working with A. K. Herrfort at his farm on our book, *Mennonite Country*, I spied an old decrepit duck or chicken crate lying broken and weathered outside a shed. Andy offered to sell it to me for five dollars and, I am sure, believed that I was nuts for even being interested in it. When I bought the crate I had no idea it would start me on a fever of furniture design. This crate, now with a base and a glass top, holds prisoner many painted chickens in my studio on Erb Street. This and several other painted pieces suggested to me the idea of trying furniture design. Through a combination of customers and friends I found myself with a deal to design some painted furniture pieces for the Lane Furniture Company of Alta Vista, Virginia.

Unfortunately, although my ideas were enthusiastically received by the Lane Company, there was a general consensus that my visions were not commercially viable. In the end the company did produce four of my cedar chest designs and I am sorry to say their estimation of their market was correct. They did not sell well. But I am so pleased that I had a chance to try my wings in another creative area. Who knows? perhaps my timing was wrong or the manufacturer was wrong or whatever. Maybe, just maybe, those ideas may some day be re-discovered.

This mural that I painted in public at the Conestoga Mall is the third in a series of large scale historical paintings. The first painting is installed in the community centre in Wellesley. The second, of the covered bridge at West Montrose, will in time find a public place somewhere in Woolwich Township. The third, of the doctor's house now the Waterlot Restaurant in New Hamburg, will be placed in some spot in Wilmot Township.

Over the years I have done a lot of painting in public. From my earlier days in Ottawa I have enjoyed this process. Lately, however, I seem to have eased, as I so often do, into another aspect of this performance art. Starting with the mural for National Trust and continuing through the Janet Lynn pieces and on to the murals for the exterior of my studio I have developed an approach to larger scale painting that is comfortable for me. It would be a lie to say that I enjoyed the trips up and down the scaffold platform. But other than showing how obviously I am out of shape, the physical problems of large scale works are minimal. It is clear that a larger work tends to grab people's attention and has some event qualities about it even though the effort may not be any greater than that for a much smaller piece.

One thing leads to another. The travel across Canada that we did for the National Trust mural led to many paintings describing various areas of this country. Some of those paintings from across Canada were united for a calendar produced by Home Hardware in 1996. It is almost impossible for me to fathom producing 400,000 copies of anything. I was there, however, beside the house-sized printing press at 3 a.m. as that giant spit out calendars so fast.

The poster for the International Plowing Match is flanked by posters for the Ontario Agricultural Museum at Milton (left) and the Ontario Conservation Authorities (right).

The art of the poster seems to have fallen on hard times. I am drawn to posters by artists such as Toulouse-Lautrec, the Leyendeckers and Norman Rockwell, but never really contemplated doing one myself. My first poster happened because the committee from the International Plowing Match at Ayr approached me. The success of that piece spawned the poster for the Ontario Agricultural Museum at Milton. I had for over ten years been involved in an on-and-off way with that facility. The art work for that piece was sponsored by the North Waterloo Farmers Mutual Insurance Co. Because of my interest in old time agriculture I was pleased to get more involved. I now sit on the board of this newly privatised institution. My latest poster was produced to celebrate fifty years of the Conservation Authorities of Ontario. Given my long association with Grand Valley Conservation Foundation, I was pleased to be asked by the Ausable Bayfield Conservation Authority to produce a painting for this purpose.

The Royal Viking Sun *was the ship that carried us through the Panana Canal.*

It really seems almost impossible that after the terrible experience that I had with sea sickness on our honeymoon trip, I should end up doing as many cruises as we have. It is unfortunate that I had not had any real horseback riding experience before that first trans-Atlantic crossing. A few years of hunter-jumper lessons taught me to absorb the motion of the ocean. Besides cruising the Caribbean and the Atlantic on holiday, we have travelled from Florida to California via the Panama Canal, along the coast of Alaska and around the British Isles as "Pied Piper" for a number of travel agencies. On these trips I paint the ports of call and generally hope to add to the enjoyment of the passengers by painting on the ship. I hope that we get further opportunities in this area.

These sketches are typical of the travel work that I do; Cabo San Lucas, Mexico (left) Sitka, Alaska (right).

Like so many other people, I came under the spell of Norman Rockwell when I was a small child. A high point in my week was the trek to downtown Waterloo, just four blocks away, to pick up the *Saturday Evening Post*. Besides Rockwell, the *Post* displayed paintings by other American illustrators. When I became a teenager and started to paint I was much taken by American illustrator/artists from an earlier time. People like the Leyendecker Brothers, Howard Pyle, Rockwell, Kent and N. C. Wyeth expanded my eyes to possibilities of visual story telling. Next for me were British artists whose works appeared in *Studio* magazine. Always present in my heart and mind was M. F. Kousal, whose early instruction shaped not only my painting, but also my idea of an artist. Through my studies at art college I found much to recommend the French Impressionists as well as their American counterparts, The Hudson River School. Their devotion to landscape predated the love of land of the Group of Seven here in Canada. I am constantly resmitten with the wonderfully lush brushwork of John Singer Sargent, Terrence Cuneo, Edward Seago and Sir Alfred Munnings. I must also mention Adrian Dingle and Hilton Hassell whose works were so prominent in Toronto in the sixties and seventies. Every time that we visit the Royal Academy Show in London, England, I find myself challenged by the range of outstanding representational painting that I find there. I have also enjoyed the work of Richard Schmid from Chicago and British painters such as David Gentleman and Bernard Dunston, not much known here.

The list of people who have affected my work is almost endless and ongoing. To the man they have given me a special gift - pleasure.

How fortunate I was to meet Terrence Cuneo at his studio in London in 1991. This little man is still active in the art world in his late 80's. It rather gives one hope.

The painting, far right, shows one of the harbours at Key West. For six years we have been fortunate enough to spend a good deal of the winter in Key West. The ambiance of this shabby little side show at the edge of the continent seems to suit our taste. Since most of my work is constructed from photos, it is possible for me to take files to Florida and develop paintings of Mennonite country or English countryside. When we are in Key West I am at my most productive. The phone seldom rings, the atmosphere calms, and demands are few.

A page from A New Harvest

Like actors, artists get typecast by the public. In my case people tend to think about my work in terms of Mennonites, horses, farms or historical subjects. While I am not unhappy with any of these topics, I do paint subjects far beyond those boundaries. I would like to think that in the last twenty years I have convinced some people that I can paint and do paint many other subjects from portraits to flowers, from landscape to interiors. Most of my work is executed in acrylics although I use watercolours, pastels, inks and pencils as well. My travel sketches often combine a number of these media.

When I approached composing another book, *A New Harvest*, ten years after *A Painter's Harvest*, I wanted to show a range of topics and approaches that I had dealt with over the years. I certainly did not ignore the Mennonite subjects but tried to include some of the lesser known bits of my work. I also included more personal observations and commentary. Although I feel confident in my painting, I am only gradually feeling comfortable in my writing style. I am extremely fortunate that Marilyn serves not only as my tag-team partner in life but also as my editor. I hope in the future to do more books but since I self-publish and wish to continue that way, the reality of the cost is ever present.

To me aesthetics are more important in a painting than anything else. The look of the work supersedes subject, medium, size or format. I am trying for something that is delicious to my eye. The factors of colour and design can produce a result that makes my mouth water. Of course this sensibility is personal. Not only does that feeling vary from person to person but changes for each individual over the years. Certainly background, exposure or experience are factors as well as such personal conditions as colour sensitivity. I have noticed that for myself I perceive colour just slightly differently with each eye. Those differences of perception are subtle to be sure. They certainly do occur from individual to individual. I am very much influenced by light, not just the quantity but the quality. I am totally taken with warm dramatic light. I am sure that this contributes to my desire to leave the cold half-light of winter in Ontario to go to Key West. For me, dramatic raking light enlivens anything. I do not understand the appeal of work by Colville with its flat grey illumination.

My preoccupation with this pursuit of a look or feel has given me grief over the years. Scholars do not seem to appreciate how an aesthetic could carry more weight than subject. Academics, through study, have come to know a lot about paintings but know almost nothing of the act of painting. The forging of colours and lines into a personally pleasing unit is most difficult to appreciate. I must admit I am uncomfortable even trying to describe in words that reflexive response that I have when something works for me in a painting. Perhaps to some extent I do not actually know it myself until I see such an effect. This surprise element in the painting process keeps me young as I explore my way through a painting. At any moment I may encounter some effect that brings me joy. Because I want to have that "Eureka!" type of experience I do not plan my paintings in a strict way. I do not feel obligated to follow the work to a pre-set destination. The work evolves in front of me as I add and subtract elements in a painting. After all these years of painting that kind of surprise is even more frequent; I like to think that I learn as I progress in a painting. Unfortunately, I do not find that I learn these truths once and then am able to continue to apply them. I often find that I must re-learn an idea that seemed obvious to me ten years ago.

Because of that, my work, although changing, seems to go around in circles. Every time I think that I am on an aesthetic tangent I find it is just the start of another, perhaps larger, circle.

It is quite maddening that I can never catch up to the ideal painting or visual effect. As I inch ahead in this process that aesthetic veers and retreats. As I learn more the goal does not get closer, indeed the ideal gets farther away and larger, just as the view of a room broadens as your eye gets closer to the key hole. For me, just looking in everyday life becomes a larger part of my visual enjoyment process. I do not mean a disciplined observation of life around me but rather an awareness that lets me enjoy the visual feast in a relaxed manner as my eye passes over it. Sometimes when I am painting I take off my glasses and look at a section of the paint from only inches away. At those close quarters the pieces of paint hold a decidedly abstract quality. I'm not sure why I enjoy looking at those blobs of paint but I do. For some reason those shapes of colour which at that distance have no readable meaning delight me. The dictionary defines beauty as those qualities giving pleasure to the mind or the senses. For me, that is what painting is all about.

"The arts are to be enjoyed; not doled out like medicine for the good of people's social or political health."
Sir Osbert Sitwell